Read for a Better World STEM
Student Action and Reflection Guide

T0104196

A Diverse STEM Education

Today's world is ever changing and full of problems to solve. To thrive in such a world, students need the ability to ask questions, form objectives, analyze information, and collaborate with others to arrive at answers. They also need to cultivate awareness, curiosity, and empathy toward themselves and the world around them. This guide helps grow and nurture students' interest and proficiency in STEM while promoting the broad diversity of thought that kids need in our culturally diverse society. It is a first step in their journey to becoming citizens of a more connected, innovative, and just world—and even more, it will build the skills they need to be architects of such a world.

About This Book

The activities in this book are based on Next Generation Science Standards and Common Core Math Standards for grades PreK through one. Each activity also promotes a social and emotional learning (SEL) competency from CASEL's SEL framework. Finally, all activities are inspired by the Social Justice Standards from Learning for Justice.

How It Works

The student guide activities are organized by the science and math standards they are based on. The resulting sections are subdivided into SEL competencies from CASEL's framework: Relationship Skills, Responsible Decision-Making, Self-Awareness, Self-Management, and Social Awareness. These competencies are called out with a colored tab in the upper corner of each page. Activities can be done in any order.

GEOMETRY

Social Awareness

Sign Shapes

Name the shape of each sign.

STEM and SEL

At a glance, STEM and SEL may be perceived as separate disciplines that develop different skill sets. But in reality, the disciplines are connected: students need social and emotional skills to succeed in STEM. As students' self-awareness and social awareness develop, they enhance their ability to be curious, pinpoint interests, and ask questions. With greater self-management and relationship skills, students are better equipped to set objectives, solve problems, and collaborate with peers. And when students grow their ability to make responsible decisions, they also grow their capacity for open-mindedness, analysis, and reasoned judgment. For more on SEL competencies, see the CASEL framework in the back of the book.

Social Justice Standards

Every subject, from language arts and social studies to science and math, benefits from a social justice lens. The anchor standards from Learning for Justice have four themes: identity, diversity, justice, and action. The activities in this book were shaped with these standards in mind. For more on these standards, see the inside of the back cover.

Grades PreK-1 Standards

NEXT GENERATION SCIENCE

EARTH AND HUMAN ACTIVITY

EARTH'S PLACE IN THE UNIVERSE

EARTH'S SYSTEMS

ENGINEERING DESIGN

FROM MOLECULES TO ORGANISMS: STRUCTURES AND PROCESSES

HEREDITY: INHERITANCE AND VARIATION OF TRAITS

MOTION AND STABILITY: FORCES AND INTERACTIONS

WAVES AND THEIR APPLICATIONS IN TECHNOLOGIES FOR INFORMATION TRANSFER

Grades PreK-1 Standards

COMMON CORE MATH

COUNTING & CARDINALITY

GEOMETRY

MEASUREMENT & DATA

NUMBER & OPERATIONS IN BASE 10

OPERATIONS & ALGEBRAIC THINKING

Color a Kinara

Kwanzaa is a celebration of African heritage. It lasts seven days. People celebrate by lighting candles on a kinara. The candle colors have special meanings. Follow the directions below to color the kinara candles!

1. The 3 candles on the left are red. They represent the challenges faced by people of African heritage.

2. The 1 middle candle is black. It represents people of African heritage.

3. The 3 candles on the right are green. They represent the earth!

How many candles does the kinara have? _____

Answers on p. 126.

Candle Counting

Each night of Kwanzaa, a new candle is lit. Kinara candles are often lit in a special order. The black candle is lit first. Then the rest of the candles are usually lit in order from left to right.

Damon is lighting candles for his family's Kwanzaa celebration. Draw flames on the candles below for each day of Kwanzaa.

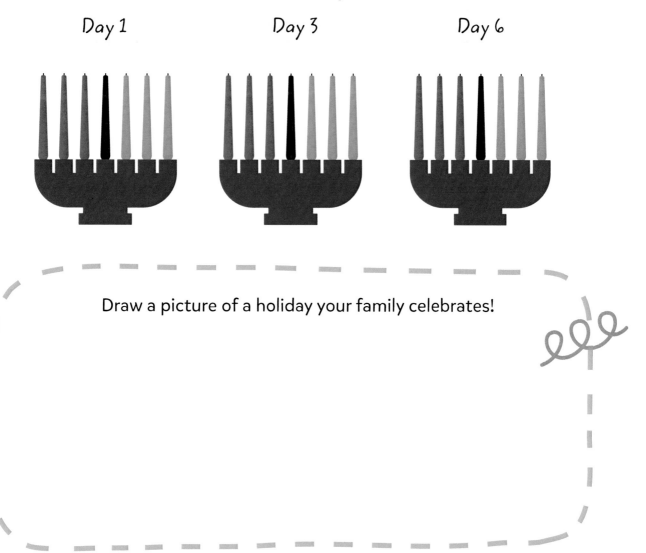

Day 1   Day 3   Day 6

Draw a picture of a holiday your family celebrates!

Answers on p. 126.

Counting through the Seasons

Celebrating Spring

Spring is a time when flowers bloom and many baby animals are born. People around the world celebrate spring in different ways.

People in Japan celebrate spring with cherry blossom festivals. Count the cherry blossoms.

In India, many people celebrate Holi, a festival of colors. Count the colored powders.

Nowruz is a holiday that marks the Iranian new year. People celebrate by decorating a table with foods, including apples. Count the apples.

Seasons Here and There

Seasons take place at different times around the world. Some places have four seasons: winter, spring, fall, and summer. Others have two: rainy and dry.

Answers on p. 126.

Summer Fun

Summer is a time when the weather is warm and the days are long. People gather for outdoor fun and festivals.

In Mongolia, people gather for a festival called Naadam. Athletes compete in horse racing. Circle 4 horses.

In Buenos Aires, Argentina, dancers compete in the city's Tango Festival. Circle 9 dancing shoes.

June is Pride Month across North America. People celebrate the LGBTQ community with rainbow-themed decorations. Circle 7 rainbows.

In China, people gather for the Dragon Boat Festival. Teams race in long boats. Circle 3 dragon heads.

What are the warm seasons like where you live? _____

_____

Fall Festivities

Fall is a time when the weather turns colder in many places around the world. People harvest crops and prepare for winter. In the Northern Hemisphere, fall takes place between September and December. In the Southern Hemisphere, fall takes place between March and June.

_____

_____

In Mexico, many people celebrate fall with Día de los Muertos. Count the sugar skulls.

In India, many people celebrate Diwali by lighting lamps called *diyas*. Count the *diyas*.

_____

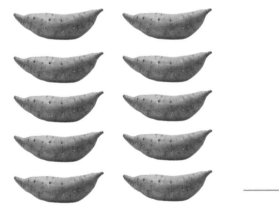

_____

In the United States, many people celebrate fall by carving pumpkins. Count the pumpkins.

In Ghana, people celebrate the yam harvest with a Festival of Yams. Count the yams.

What is your favorite season? _____

_____

Answers on p. 126.

Winter Traditions

In many places around the world, winter is a time of cold weather and long nights. In the Northern Hemisphere, winter takes place between December and March. In the Southern Hemisphere, winter takes place between June and August.

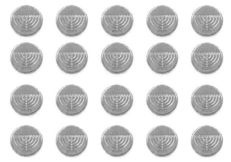

Lunar New Year is one of China's most important holidays. People celebrate by lighting fireworks. Circle 14 fireworks.

Hanukkah is an eight-day Jewish holiday during which people give presents like gelt coins. Circle 8 gelt coins.

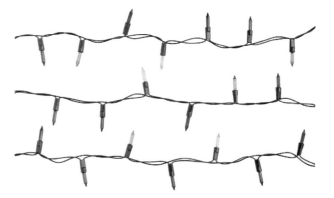

In Puerto Rico, many people celebrate Three Kings Day in early January. Circle 11 crowns.

Christmas is celebrated by many people in North America and Europe. Circle 15 Christmas lights.

What is your favorite family tradition? _____

More or Fewer Letters?

Meet the kids in Deja's class. Which student has more letters in their name?

Amaya

Ari

_____ has more letters in their name.

How many letters does that student have? _____

Dolores

Nekima

_____ has more letters in their name.

How many letters does that student have? _____

Mohammed

Sofia

_____ has more letters in their name.

How many letters does that student have? _____

Write your name below!

_____

How many letters are in your name?

Answers on p. 126.

Community Counting

Read about some of the helpers you may see in your community. Then, count the number of items each helper is using!

Jess is a letter carrier. How many letters does he have?_____

Ibrahaim is a firefighter. How many helmets does his fire station have?

_____

Lili is a city bus driver. How many stops does her bus route have? _____

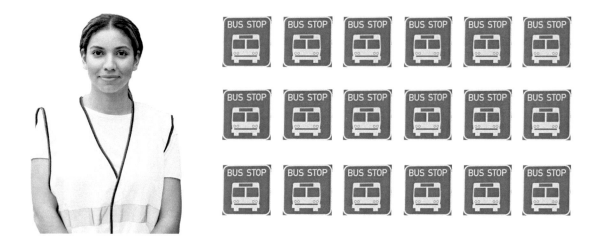

Jaxon is a nurse. How many bandages does he have? _____

Circle the pictures of any helpers you see in your community.

What other helpers do you see in your community? _____

Answers on p. 126.

Totem Poles by Tens

The Haida are a Native American people in the United States and Canada. The Haida are known for their totem poles. These are tall logs with faces carved into the wood. They tell stories of important events and people.

Count by tens to connect the dots and finish the totem pole drawing.

© 2023 Lerner Publishing Group

Answers on p. 126.

Draw a totem pole that represents your family below!

How Many?

Count the objects in each picture!

How many candles are on the Hanukkah menorah?

_____ candles

How many tomatoes does Christina have?

_____ tomatoes

How many cookies are on Leah's pan?

_____ cookies

How many Diwali gifts does this family have?

_____ gifts

How many tortillas are cooking on the pan?

_____ tortillas

Answers on p. 126.

Who Has More?

Circle the missing piece of each sentence.

Jordan   Gloria

Jordan has

more carrots than /

fewer carrots than /

the same number of carrots as

Gloria.

Layla   Melani

Layla has

more cards than /

fewer cards than /

the same number of cards as

Melani.

Dhia has

more flags than /

fewer flags than /

the same number of flags as

Jana.

Francisca

Francisca's teacher

Francisca has

more books than /

fewer books than /

the same number of books as

her teacher.

© 2023 Lerner Publishing Group

Answers on p. 126.

Healthy Food Shapes

Healthy foods help keep your body and mind working well. Circle the healthy food below that looks most like the shape shown in the box!

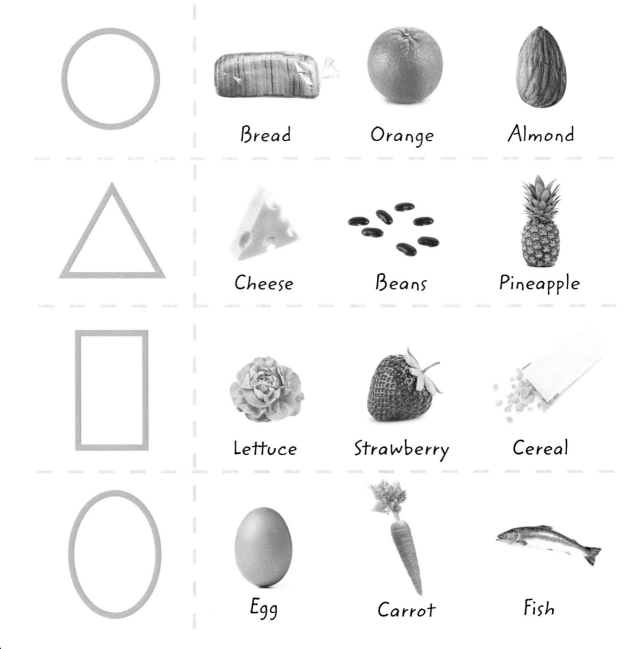

Bread   Orange   Almond

Cheese   Beans   Pineapple

Lettuce   Strawberry   Cereal

Egg   Carrot   Fish

Answers on p. 126.

Decorate the shapes below to make them look like healthy foods. Cut them out and combine them to make a healthy meal on page 25.

My Meal

Use the shapes you cut out to make a healthy meal below!

What is your favorite healthy food? _____

No Shape Like Home

Homes come in many different shapes and sizes. What shapes do you see in the homes below?

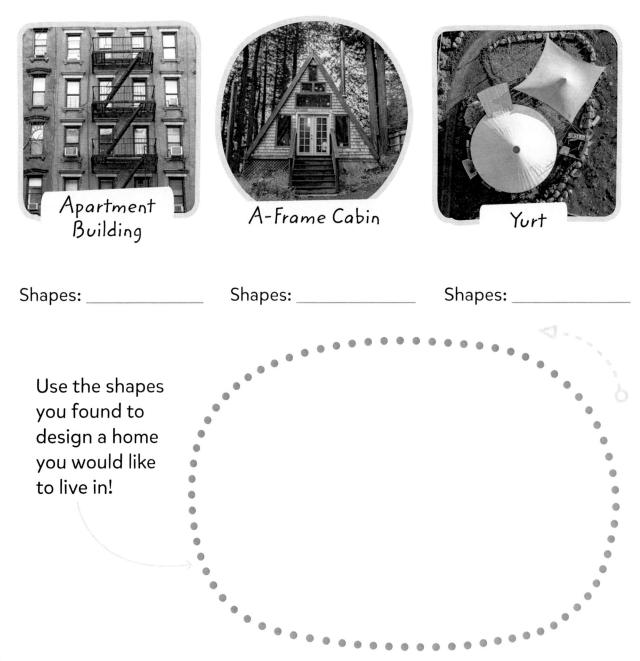

Apartment Building

A-Frame Cabin

Yurt

Shapes: _____

Shapes: _____

Shapes: _____

Use the shapes you found to design a home you would like to live in!

Answers on p. 126.

Sharing Fairly

Draw lines to cut these foods into equal pieces for sharing.

Cut the injera bread into
two equal pieces.

Cut the pizza into
four equal pieces.

Cut the pecan pie into
quarters.

Cut the tortilla into halves.

Answers on p. 126.

Over, Under, More

Circle the word that fills in each sentence.

Nina is behind / above / below her mom.

The girl in blue is below / above / behind the girl in yellow.

Christopher stands behind / in front of / beside Marcus.

Tevy sits behind / above / in front of her mom.

Imani's dad sits behind / below / in front of Imani.

Keiko sits in front of / behind / next to her teacher.

Answers on p. 126.

Draw the Shape

Draw the shape you see in each picture.

Draw the shape of Melody's book.

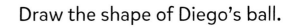

Draw the shape of Diego's ball.

Draw the shape of the flags
behind Lei.

Draw the shape of Gabriella's gift.

Draw the shape of Natalia's watermelon.

Draw the shape of Sabri's kite.

Answers on p. 126.

Sign Shapes

Name the shape of each sign.

_____

_____

_____

 Answers on p. 126.

Country Flags

Find the shapes in the country flags!

Which flags have circles? _____

Which flags have squares? _____

Which flags have triangles? _____

Which flags have rectangles? _____

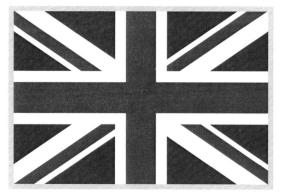

Flag of the United Kingdom

Flag of Chile

Flag of Niger

Flag of Liberia

Answers on p. 126.

Family Flag

Draw a flag that represents your family. Include in the flag at least one rectangle, one square, one triangle, and one circle.

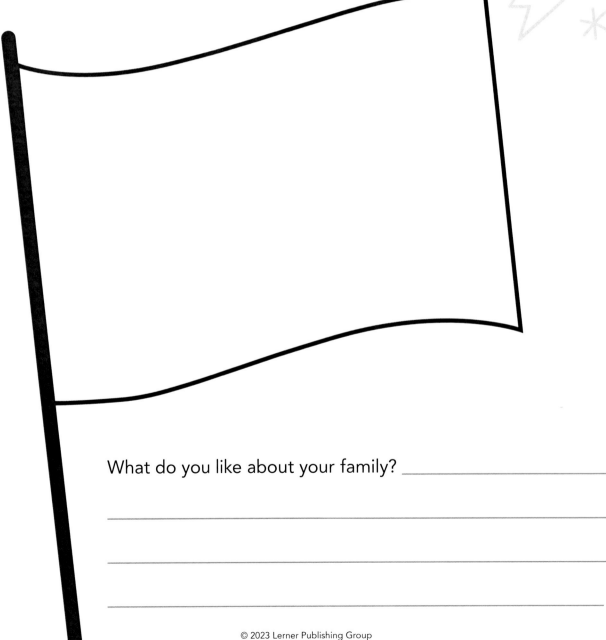

What do you like about your family? _____

_____

_____

_____

Pizza Party

Build your own pizza using the toppings shown below, or pick your own! Then cut out the pizza and use it to answer the questions on page 37.

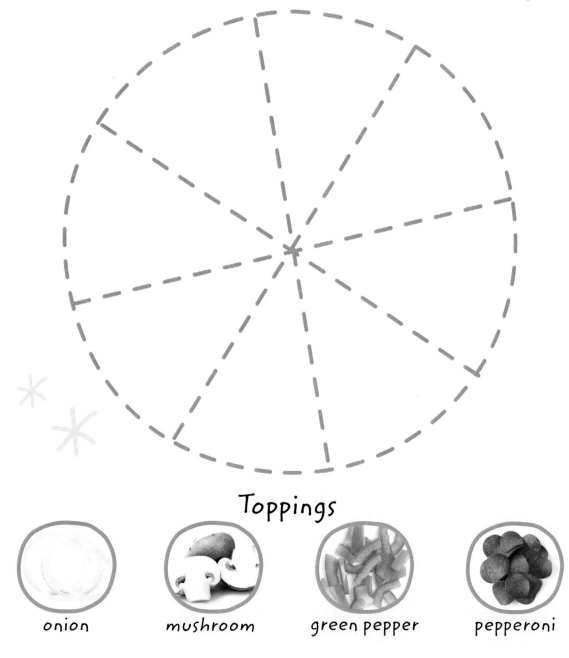

Toppings

onion   mushroom   green pepper   pepperoni

Cut the pizza into slices along the dotted lines. Imagine you are having a pizza party with some friends. Use the pizza cutouts to answer the questions below.

1. If you share the pizza equally with one friend, how many pieces will each of you get?

2. If you eat ¼ of the pizza, how many pieces did you eat?

3. If you eat ¼ of the pizza and your friends eat ½ of the pizza, how many pieces are left?

4. How many people could share the pizza so everyone gets a slice?

Answers on p. 126.

Spot the Differences

Ramadan is a special month for Muslims. People hang lanterns during Ramadan. Circle three differences between the lanterns below!

Día de los Muertos is a Mexican holiday. People eat candy shaped like skulls. They also paint skulls on their faces. Circle three differences between the skulls below!

Tangram Creations

A tangram is a puzzle that was invented in China. Cut out the seven shapes of the tangram puzzle on the next page. Make the shapes on page 43 out of tangram pieces. Draw how you made each shape!

Example:

This square is made up of one large triangle and two smaller triangles.

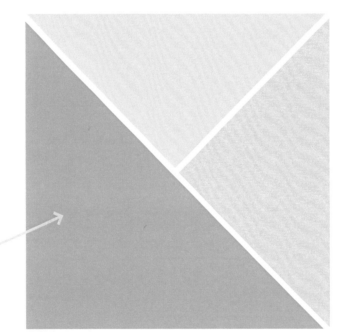

Cut out the tangram puzzle pieces below.

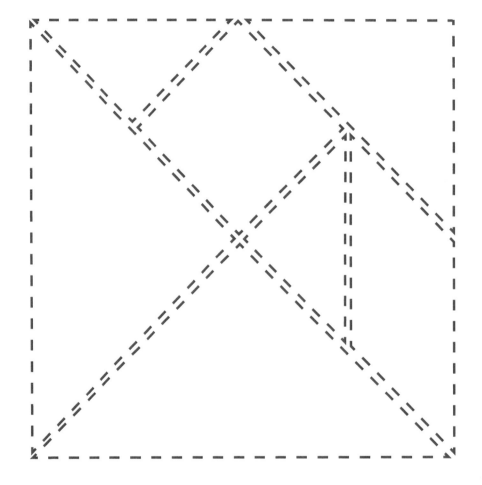

Use the tangram puzzle pieces to make the shapes below.

Comparing Creatures

Endangered animals are creatures that are at risk of dying out. Learn about some endangered animals from around the world and compare them!

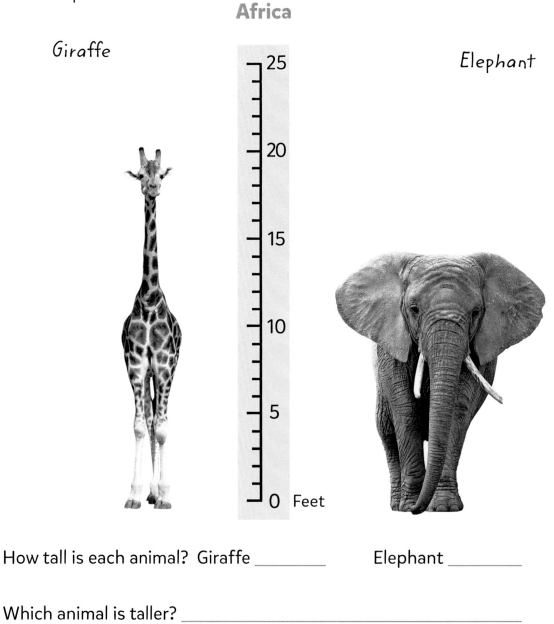

Africa

Giraffe

Elephant

25

20

15

10

5

0 Feet

How tall is each animal? Giraffe _____   Elephant _____

Which animal is taller? _____

South America

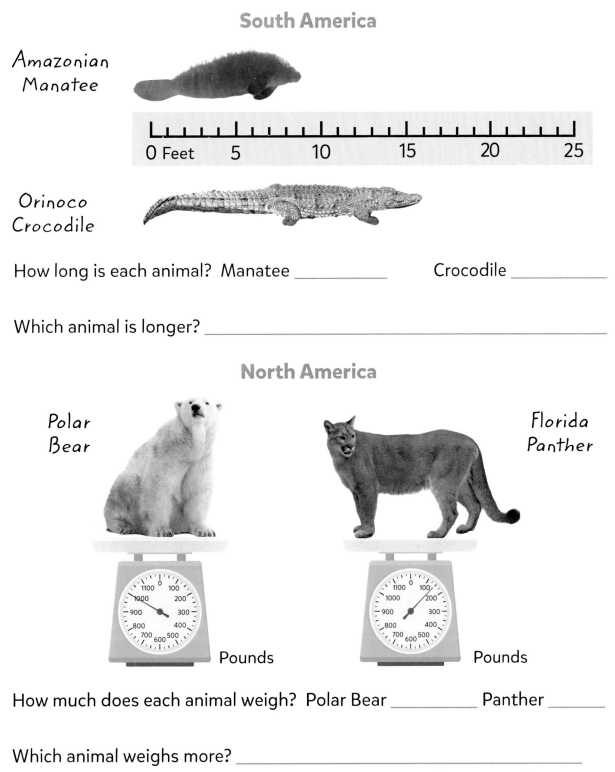

Amazonian
Manatee

0 Feet   5   10   15   20   25

Orinoco
Crocodile

How long is each animal? Manatee _____   Crocodile _____

Which animal is longer? _____

North America

Polar
Bear

Florida
Panther

Pounds   Pounds

How much does each animal weigh? Polar Bear _____ Panther _____

Which animal weighs more? _____

Answers on p. 126.

© 2023 Lerner Publishing Group

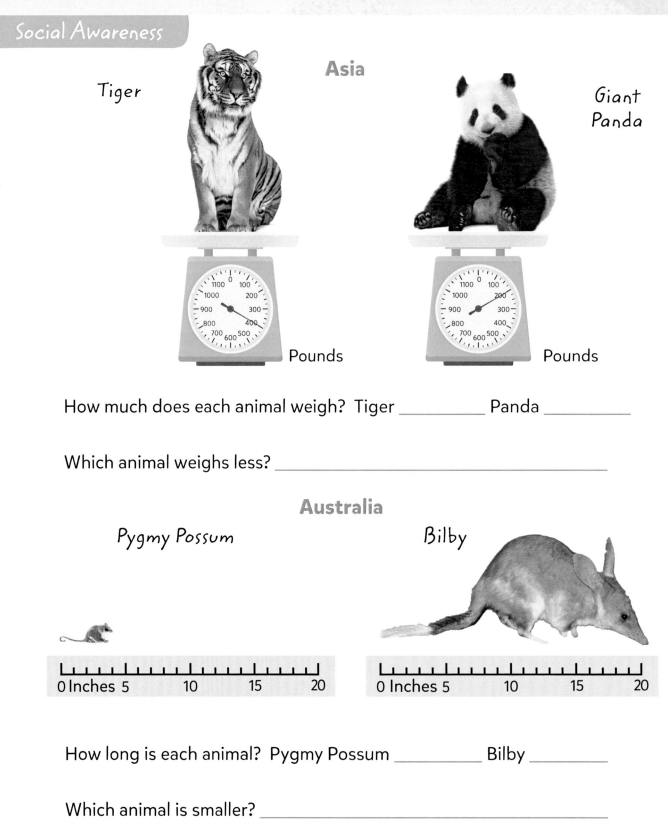

Asia

Tiger

Giant Panda

Pounds   Pounds

How much does each animal weigh? Tiger _____ Panda _____

Which animal weighs less? _____

Australia

Pygmy Possum

Bilby

0 Inches 5   10   15   20   0 Inches 5   10   15   20

How long is each animal? Pygmy Possum _____ Bilby _____

Which animal is smaller? _____

Europe

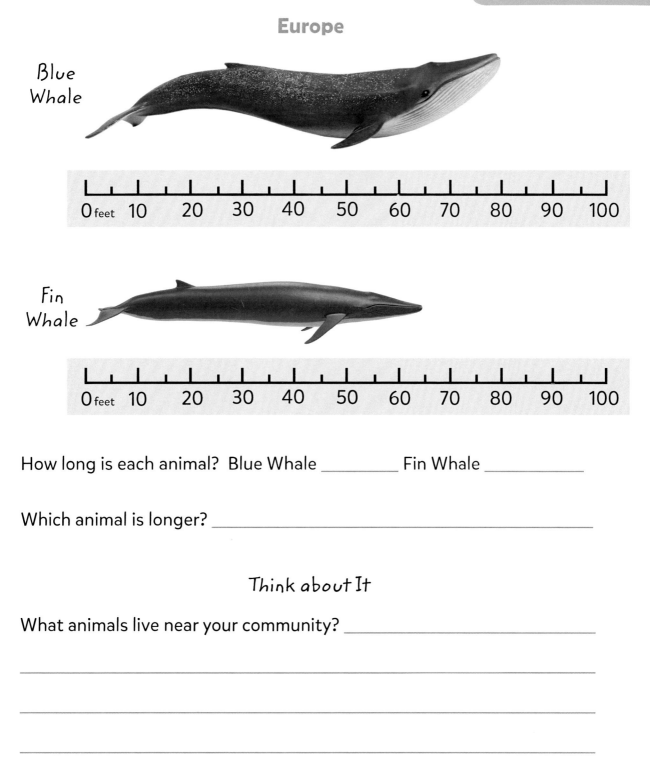

Blue
Whale

Fin
Whale

How long is each animal? Blue Whale _____ Fin Whale _____

Which animal is longer? _____

Think about It

What animals live near your community? _____

_____

_____

_____

Answers on p. 126.

Josie's Juneteenth

Juneteenth is an American holiday. It honors June 19, 1865. This was the day enslaved Black people in Galveston, Texas, learned they were free. Learn how Josie celebrates Juneteenth. Write what time each activity takes place below.

Parade

Time: _____

Juneteenth Festival

Time: _____

Family Barbecue

Time: _____

Fireworks

Time: _____

Answers on p. 126.

Time to Celebrate!

What is a holiday that you celebrate? Draw pictures below showing what you might be doing during the times shown on the clocks.

Holiday name: _____

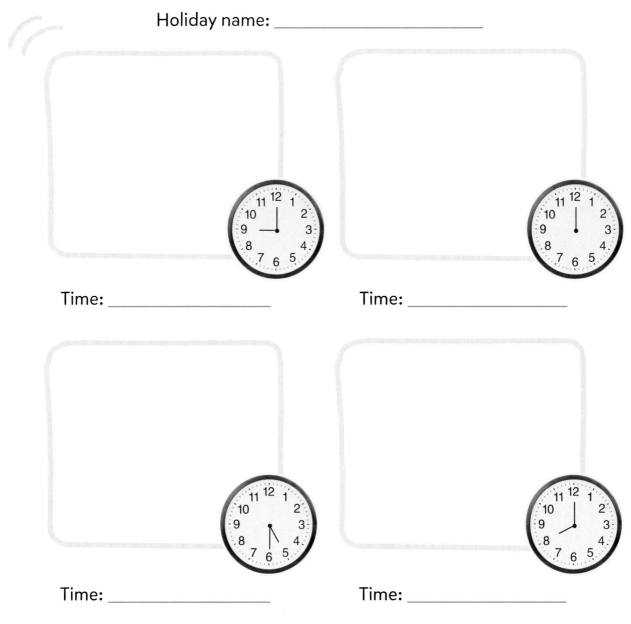

Time: _____   Time: _____

Time: _____   Time: _____

Length & Weight

Movement is healthy for your body and mind. Sports and games are a great way to get moving and have fun! Compare the sports objects below.

Baseball

Cricket Ball

Ounces

Ounces

Which ball is heavier? _____

Tennis Racket

Ping-Pong Paddle

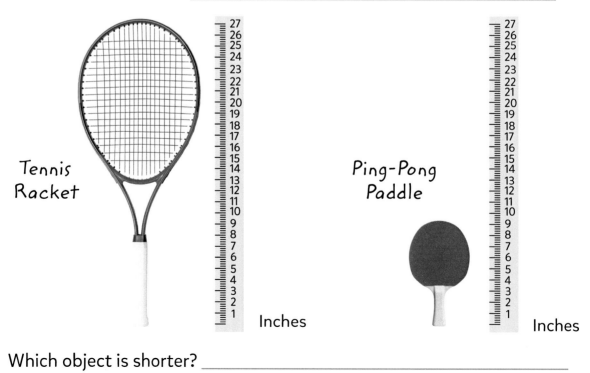

Inches

Inches

Which object is shorter? _____

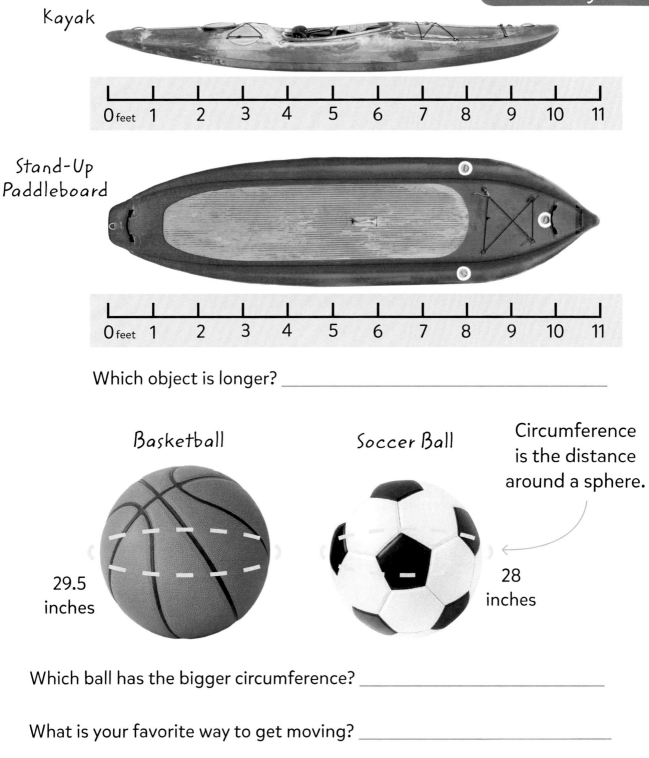

Kayak

| 0 feet | 1 | 2 | 3 | 4 | 5 | 6 | 7 | 8 | 9 | 10 | 11 |

Stand-Up Paddleboard

| 0 feet | 1 | 2 | 3 | 4 | 5 | 6 | 7 | 8 | 9 | 10 | 11 |

Which object is longer? _____

Basketball

Soccer Ball

Circumference is the distance around a sphere.

29.5 inches

28 inches

Which ball has the bigger circumference? _____

What is your favorite way to get moving? _____

_____

Answers on p. 126.   **51**

We Are Different!

Circle the correct word that fills in each sentence.

My grandpa is bigger / smaller than me.

My granddaughter is bigger / smaller than me.

I am shorter / taller than my grandson.

I am shorter / taller than my grandma.

I am
heavier / lighter
than my mom.

I am
heavier / lighter
than my daughter.

My arm is
thinner / thicker
than my dad's.

My arm is
thinner / thicker
than my son's.

My hair is
longer / shorter
than my sister's.

My hair is
longer / shorter
than my brother's.

Answers on p. 127.

Kitchen Cleanup

Mikala is putting away items in her kitchen. Color in the units below each object. Then write how long the object is.

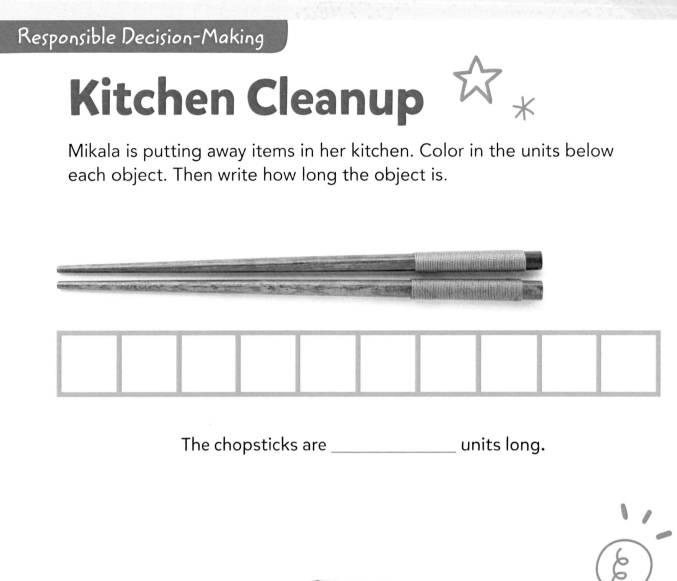

The chopsticks are _____ units long.

The fork is _____ units long.

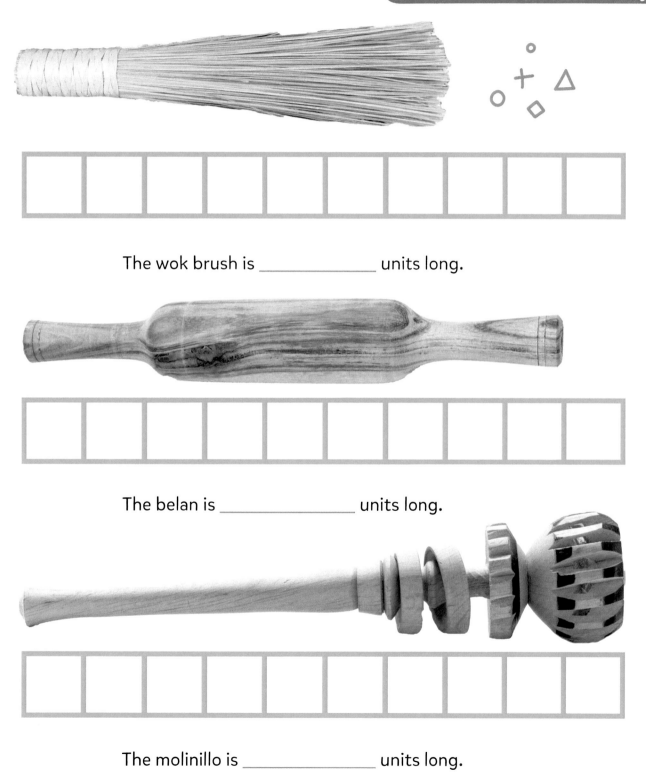

The wok brush is _____ units long.

The belan is _____ units long.

The molinillo is _____ units long.

Answers on p. 127.

How We Go to School

The graph below shows how Cicely and her classmates get to school. Use the graph to answer the questions on the next page.

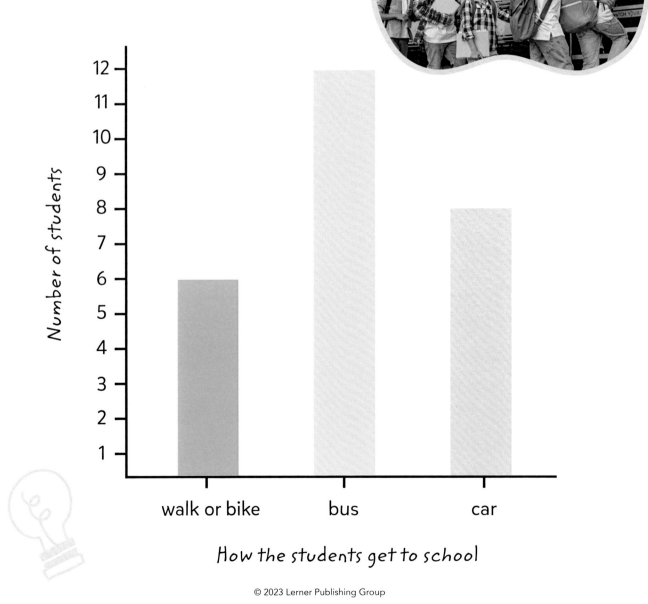

How many students walk or bike to school? _____

How many students take the bus to school? _____

How many students go to school in a car? _____

What is the total number of students in Cicely's class? _____

How many more students take the bus than ride in a car? _____

How many fewer students walk or bike than take a car? _____

Answers on p. 127.

Holi Colors

Holi is a Hindu holiday. It celebrates the start of spring. People celebrate Holi by throwing colored powder and spraying colored water on each other. Different colors have different meanings. Color the picture on page 59 with the colors below. Each color gets a number. Solve the equations to find out which numbers are assigned to each color.

$$10 + 10 = \text{blue}$$

$$30 + 10 = \text{red}$$

$$60 + 10 = \text{yellow}$$

$$70 - 10 = \text{green}$$

$$20 - 10 = \text{orange}$$

$$40 - 10 = \text{purple}$$

What is your favorite color?

_____

Holi Color Meanings

blue: the Hindu god Krishna

red: love

yellow: knowledge, happiness, and peace

green: nature and new beginnings

orange: a new day

purple: magic

Happy Harvest Place Value

Harvest time is when crops are ripe and farmers harvest them. This takes place at different times around the world. Learn about some of the important crops harvested in different countries! Count how many of each crop there is in tens and ones.

Peru

Cassava

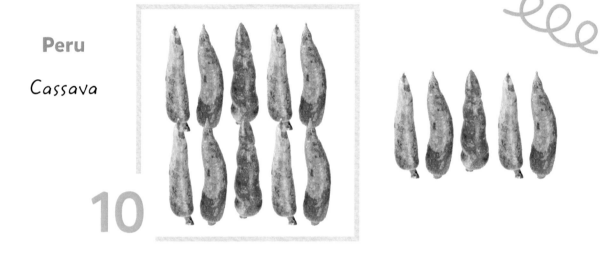

Tens: _____   Ones: _____

Egypt

Watermelons

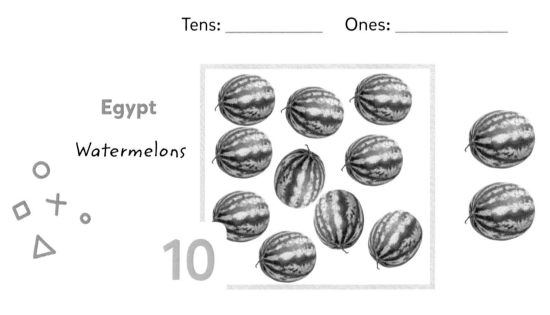

Tens: _____   Ones: _____

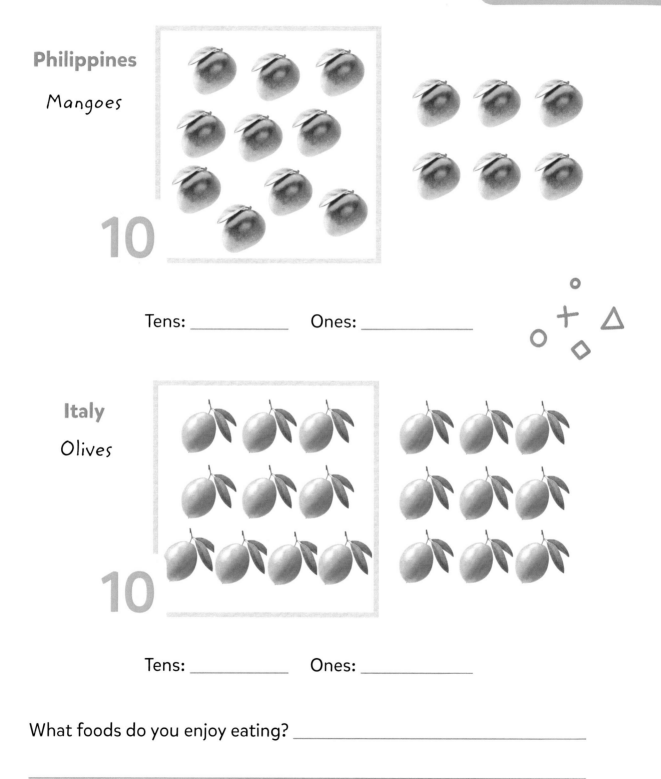

Philippines

Mangoes

10

Tens: _____   Ones: _____

Italy

Olives

10

Tens: _____   Ones: _____

What foods do you enjoy eating? _____

_____

Answers on p. 127.

Cami Counts Seeds

Cami and her neighbors are planting a community vegetable garden. Complete the number pattern to see how many seeds she plants in each garden bed.

Carrots

3   [ ]   1   3   2

Tomatoes

2   4   3   2   [ ]

Pumpkins

1   [ ]   1   5   1

Cabbage

| 10 | | 10 | 5 | 10 |

Green Beans

| | 4 | 2 | 1 | 4 |

What plants would you put in your garden bed? Draw them in the bed below!

Tracking Tortillas

Lupé helps his grandma sell tortillas at the farmers market. He keeps track of how many tortillas they sell. He draws a line for every ten tortillas and a circle for every one tortilla.

Write the number that goes with each group of lines and circles.

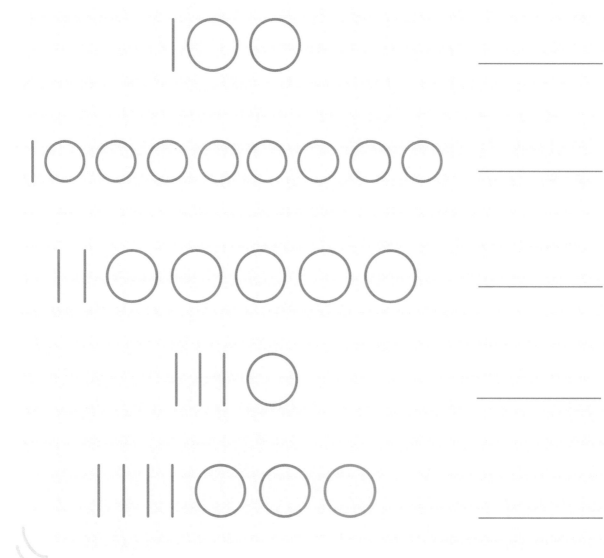

Now draw lines and circles that represent the numbers below.

7 _____

15 _____

23 _____

37 _____

44 _____

Answers on p. 127.

Community Garden Math

Nhia and his grandma grow food in their community garden. This is a garden that the neighborhood shares. Use adding and subtracting to answer the questions about Nhia's community garden.

1. Nhia counts six tomatoes growing on his tomato plant. His grandma counts five tomatoes growing on her tomato plant. How many tomatoes are growing on their plants?

2. Ms. Lor grew 12 ears of corn. She gave 5 of them to Mr. Fritz. How many ears of corn does Ms. Lor have left?

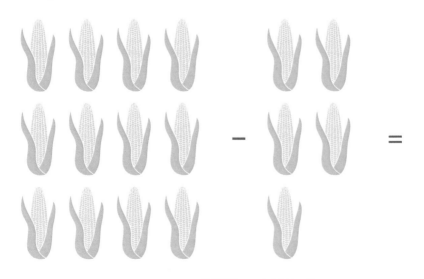

3. Nhia plants 9 carrot seeds. His friend Tawni plants 7 carrot seeds. How many carrot seeds did they plant in total?

4. Nhia and his neighbors filled 14 baskets with green beans from the garden. They gave 9 baskets to help feed local families. How many baskets did they have left?

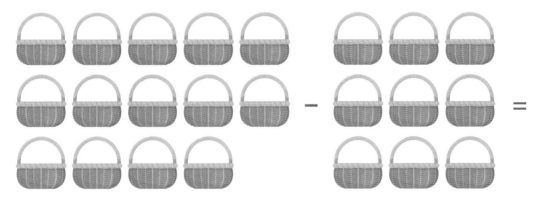

5. Nhia's grandma and her friend grew 13 pumpkins. They used 8 pumpkins to make pumpkin pies for the community. How many pumpkins did they have left?

Answers on p. 127.

✳ Finger Math

Help these kids add and subtract the numbers they are holding up on their fingers.

  = _____

_____   _____

 −  = _____

_____   _____

Relationship Skills

+ = _____

_____   _____

− = _____

_____   _____

+ = _____

_____   _____

Answers on p. 127.

Diwali Sweets

Diwali is an important holiday in India and other countries. Kiaan is making sweets for Diwali. Draw how many more of each sweet Kiaan needs so he has ten of each. Then write the number of sweets he needs.

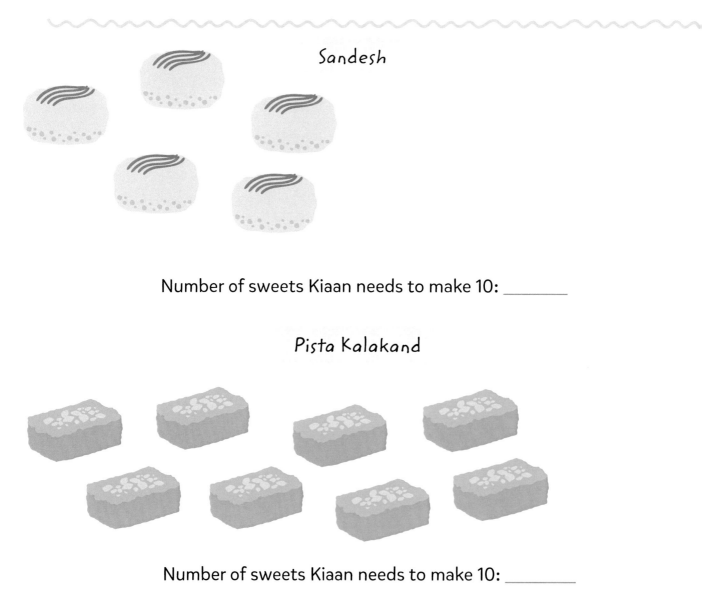

Sandesh

Number of sweets Kiaan needs to make 10: _____

Pista Kalakand

Number of sweets Kiaan needs to make 10: _____

Peda

Number of sweets Kiaan needs to make 10: _____

Mysore Pak

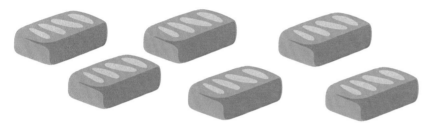

Number of sweets Kiaan needs to make 10: _____

Rose Ladoo

Number of sweets Kiaan needs to make 10: _____

Gulab Jamun

Number of sweets Kiaan needs to make 10: _____

Answers on p. 127.

Helping Hand Math

Add and subtract to solve these problems about kids helping out!

1. Martin helped his dad wash the dishes after dinner. Martin washed 4 dishes. His dad washed 5 dishes. How many dishes did they wash in total?

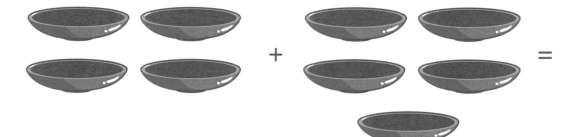

2. Raj and Meera helped their grandma hang clothes up to dry. Raj hung 3 shirts. Meera hung 4 shirts. Grandma hung 5 shirts. How many shirts did they hang in total?

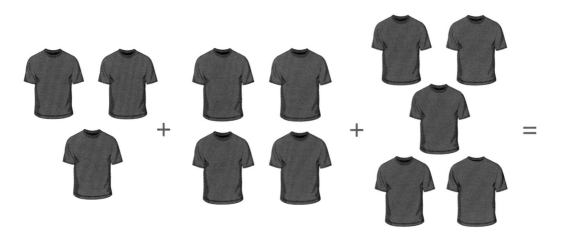

3. Aatifa helped hang signs for the school bake sale. There were 15 signs to hang. Aatifa hung 7 signs. How many signs were left?

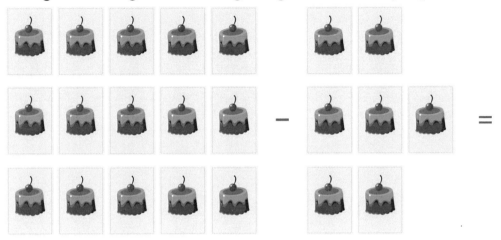

4. Xin collected 6 cans of soup to give to local families. Nel collected 4 cans. Lupé collected 8. How many cans of soup did they collect in total?

5. Cho helped her aunt make 16 rice cakes. They ate 4 rice cakes right away. How many rice cakes were left?

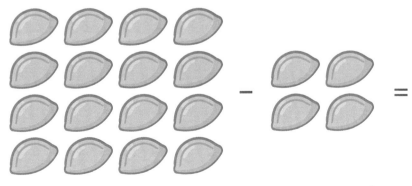

Answers on p. 127.

Visit a Coral Reef!

Coral reefs are important homes to many ocean plants and animals.

Circle these creatures in the coral reef picture!

Angelfish

Lionfish

Parrotfish

Butterflyfish

Brain Coral

Answers on p. 127.

A coral reef is an ecosystem. An ecosystem is a community of plants and animals that rely on one another to survive. Draw a picture of an ecosystem near you.

Draw pictures of some of the plants and animals in your ecosystem.

_____ _____ _____ _____

Reduce, Reuse, Recycle!

Before you throw something away, remember the three Rs.

Reduce means to make less waste by using less.

Draw a circle around the picture that shows reducing.

Reuse means to use something again or find a new use for something.

Draw a square around the picture that shows reusing.

Recycle means turning something used into something new.

Draw a star around the picture that shows recycling.

Bring your own bag to the store so you don't have to use a plastic bag.

Wear used clothing instead of buying new clothing.

Put plastic, glass, and paper products in a recycling bin.

Answers on p. 127.

Responsible Decision-Making

Draw a poster to remind others to reduce, reuse, and recycle. Then cut it out and hang it where people will see it!

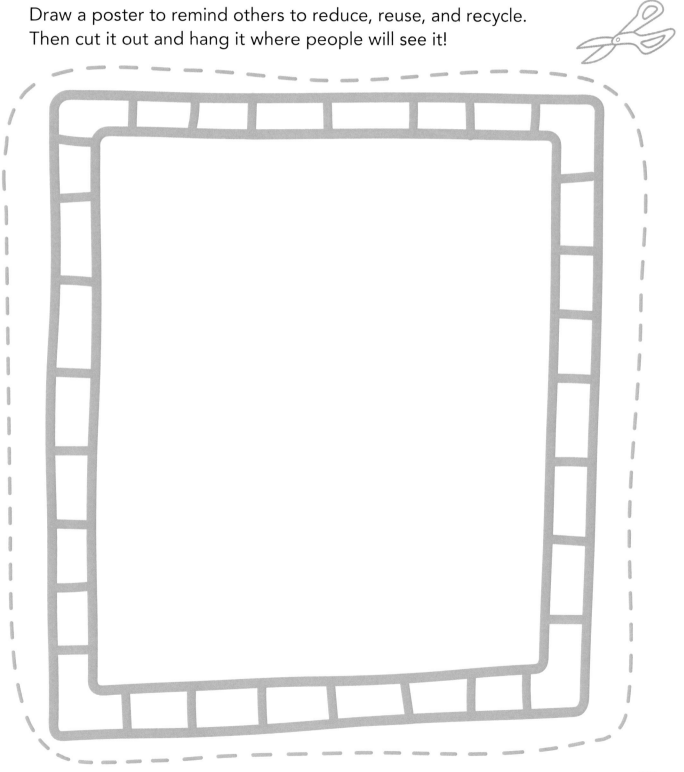

Responsible Decision-Making

Pueblo Homes

The Pueblo are a Native American people. They live in the desert. The weather is hot and dry in the desert.

Pueblo homes are made of clay. The clay keeps the homes cool in the desert.

This is a Pueblo home.

Your home protects you from weather. Draw a picture of your home here!

All Kinds of Plants

Plants live in all kinds of places around the world.

Circle the plants in the pictures below.

Draw a star next to the plants you see most where you live!

Answers on p. 127.

Severe Weather Flash Cards

Sometimes the weather causes strong storms. Cut out the flash cards below and write the type of weather on the back. Use them to remember different types of weather!

Responsible Decision-Making

FLOOD	LIGHTNING	SNOWSTORM
DROUGHT	HURRICANE	TORNADO

Animals in the City

Wild animals live in all kinds of places, including cities!

Circle the animals in the pictures below.

Draw a star next to the animals you see most where you live!

Answers on p. 127.

Self-Awareness

✳ Sun & Shadow

The sun seems to move across the sky throughout the day.
This is because Earth is slowly spinning as it circles the sun.

When the sun rises in the morning, Isabella's shadow is long.

When the sun is over Isabella's head, her shadow is short.

When the sun sets in the evening, Isabella's shadow is long.

✱ Go outside three times on a sunny day. Stand in the same spot each time. Circle your answer for each time of day below. Then draw a picture of yourself outside. Include where the sun is and where your shadow is.

My shadow is . . .

a) shorter than me

b) longer than me

c) as long as me

Morning

Midday

My shadow is . . .

a) shorter than me

b) longer than me

c) as long as me

My shadow is . . .

a) shorter than me

b) longer than me

c) as long as me

Evening

Social Awareness

Constellation Exploration

A constellation is a group of stars. These groups are named after patterns people saw in them. These patterns looked like animals, people, and objects.

Learn about the names and stories of some familiar constellations.

The Great Bear (Big Dipper)

According to an Iroquois legend, the rectangle-like shape of the constellation is a big bear. The remaining three stars are hunters.

Bunya (Southern Cross)

According to Aboriginal Australians, the top of the constellation is Bunya the possum's nose. His tail hangs to the left.

Osiris (Orion)

According to ancient Egyptians, this constellation shows Osiris. He is the Egyptian god of the underworld.

Create your own constellation and write a story about it below.

My Star Story

_____

_____

_____

Winter & Summer

The sun sets at different times throughout the year.

Carlos makes a table showing what time the sun sets on four days of the year.

Date	Time of Sunset
March 20	7:08 p.m.
June 20	8:31 p.m.
September 22	6:53 p.m.
December 21	4:32 p.m.

Which day had the latest sunset? _____

Which day had the earliest sunset? _____

The sun is out for longer in the _____
(summer / winter)

The sky is dark for longer in the _____
(summer / winter)

Answers on p. 127.

Draw a picture of what you do on summer evenings.

Draw a picture of what you do on winter evenings.

Moon Phases

Have you ever noticed that the moon's shape seems to change each night? The different moon shapes are called lunar phases. There are eight phases in a lunar month.

Match the English names for the moon phases with the Hawaiian names and pictures on the next page.

A) Third Quarter

B) Waning Gibbous

C) Full Moon

D) Waxing Gibbous

E) First Night of the New Moon

F) First Quarter

G) Waxing Crescent

H) Waning Crescent

I) Dark Moon

Hint!

Waxing means getting bigger.

Waning means getting smaller.

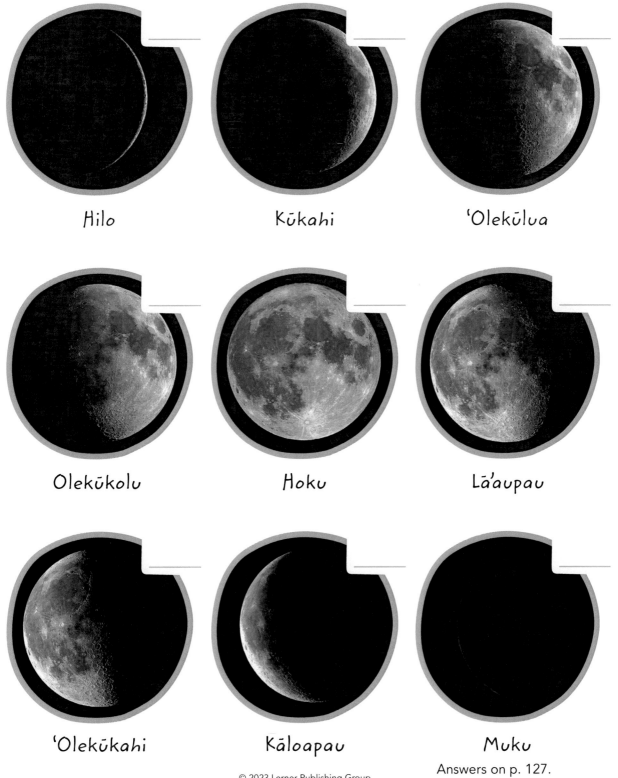

Hilo

Kūkahi

ʻOlekūlua

Olekūkolu

Hoku

Lāʻaupau

ʻOlekūkahi

Kāloapau

Muku

Answers on p. 127.

Self-Management

My Moon Journal

Look at the moon every night for the next 28 days. Shade in the circles showing how the moon looks each night. If it is cloudy, draw clouds in the frame.

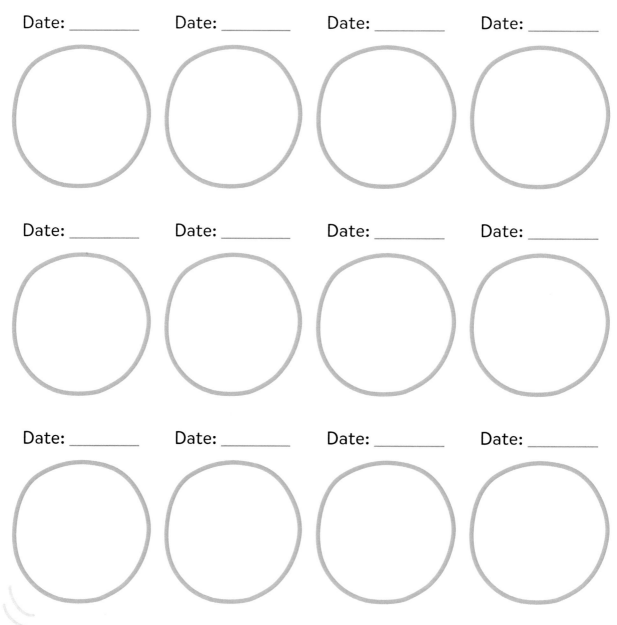

Date: _____   Date: _____   Date: _____   Date: _____

Date: _____   Date: _____   Date: _____   Date: _____

Date: _____   Date: _____   Date: _____   Date: _____

Date: _____

Date: _____

Date: _____

Date: _____

Date: _____

Date: _____

Date: _____

Date: _____

Date: _____

Date: _____

Date: _____

Date: _____

Date: _____

Date: _____

Date: _____

Date: _____

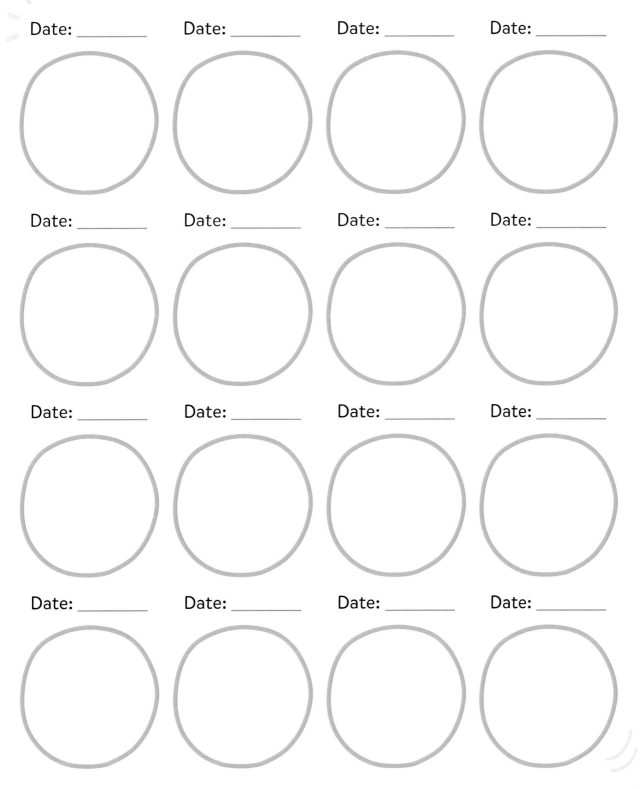

What's the Weather?

Circle the answer that best describes the weather where you live.

It is _____ where I live today.
(sunny / cloudy)

It is _____ where I live today.
(wet / dry)

It is _____ where I live today.
(windy / still)

It _____ snows where I live.
(always / sometimes / never)

Draw a dot on the scale below to describe the temperature today.

_____

cold   cool   warm   hot

Draw a picture of your favorite type of weather below. Include yourself in the picture. Show what you like to do in this weather!

My Weather

What's the weather like where you live today? Cut out the icons on the next page and use them to fill out the weather chart on page 99.

What are the seasons like where you live?

_____

_____

What kind of weather do you like best?

_____

_____

Wind

_____

Temperature

_____

Weather

_____

What I'm wearing

_____

Make your own icons!

_____

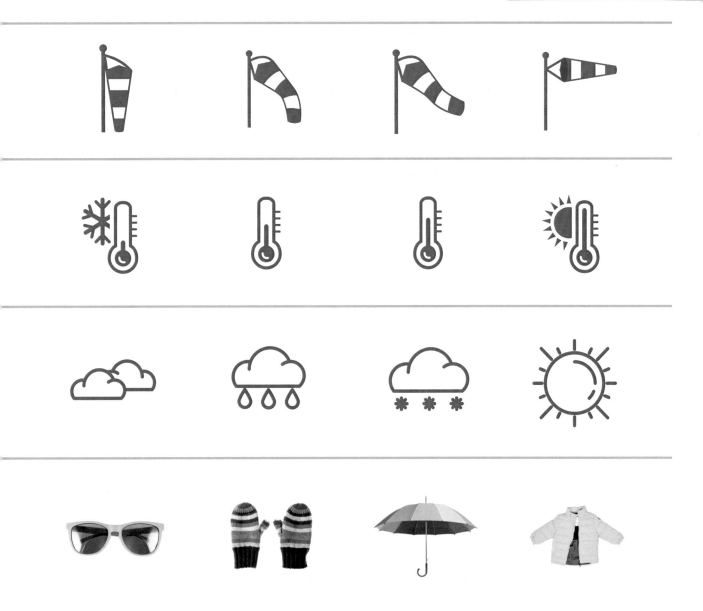

Today's Weather

✳ Weather	
Temperature	
Wind	
What I'm wearing	

Animal Engineers

The animal kingdom is full of amazing engineers. These animals build structures to help them survive. Match the structures below to their animal builders on the next page!

A.

B.

C.

D.

Termite

Weaverbird

Bee

Beaver

Have you ever seen a bird's nest or watched a squirrel burying nuts? What are some ways the animals around you change their environments?

_____

_____

_____

Answers on p. 127.

Human Engineers

Humans change their environments. These changes help humans better survive. Match the changes below with the ways they help humans on the next page.

A.

B.

☆ * C.

D.

Look around your community. What are some of the ways humans have changed your environment?

_____

_____

_____

Answers on p. 127.

Responsible Decision-Making

From Here to There

Cars were invented to help people travel far in less time. However, many cars move by burning gasoline. This is bad for our air.

Invent a new and safe way that humans could get from place to place. Draw your invention in the space below!

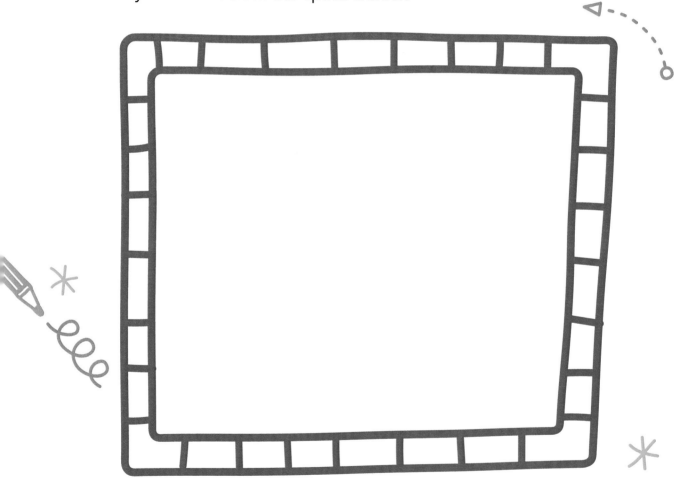

What do you call your invention? _____

_____

Bean Life Cycle

Beans are an important source of healthy food for people all over the world. Cut out the images below and put them in order on the diagram.

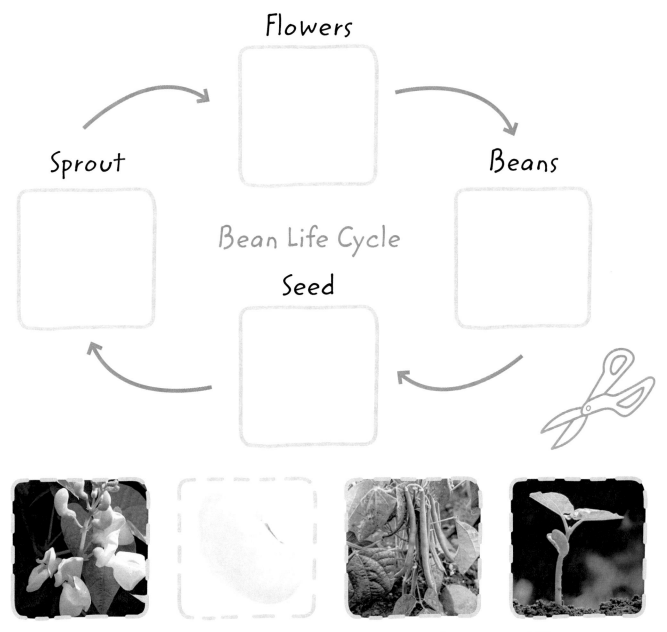

Flowers

Sprout

Beans

Bean Life Cycle

Seed

Answers on p. 127.

Self-Awareness

What is your favorite way to eat beans? *

_____

_____

_____

Draw a picture of your favorite bean dish!

What a Bean Needs

Circle the pictures showing the three things a bean needs to grow.

What helps you grow? _____

_____

_____

Answers on p. 127.

Animal Inspiration

When engineer Eiji Nakatsu was designing a new train, he looked to animals for ideas. He designed the train's front in the shape of a kingfisher beak. This made the train faster!

Kingfisher

Bullet Train

What helpful inventions could you create from animal features? Draw inventions based on each animal's feature!

Porcupine

My Invention

Sharp quills protect the animal from predators.

Tortoise

Tortoise shells are like armor that protect them from predators.

My Invention

Octopus

Octopuses can change the color of their skin to blend into their surroundings.

My Invention

What We Need

Draw lines to match the pictures of plants and animals with what they need to live.

Plant or Animal   What They Need

Answers on p. 127.

Self-Awareness

Draw some of the things you need in the space below.

Farm Visit

Read the story below about Tisha's class trip to the farm. Then answer questions about the story.

Tisha's Trip to the Farm

Tisha's class went to the farm. She saw all the animals eat. The cows ate grass. The horses ate hay. Tisha and her friend Tess liked the chickens. The girls took turns feeding grains to the chickens. Then it was time for the kids to eat too. Tisha shared her orange with Tess. They loved being at the farm!

What did the cows eat? _____

_____

What did the horses eat? _____

_____

What did the chickens eat? _____

_____

What did Tisha share with Tess? _____

_____

Answers on p. 127.

Food for My Body

On the plate below, draw three foods that you often eat.

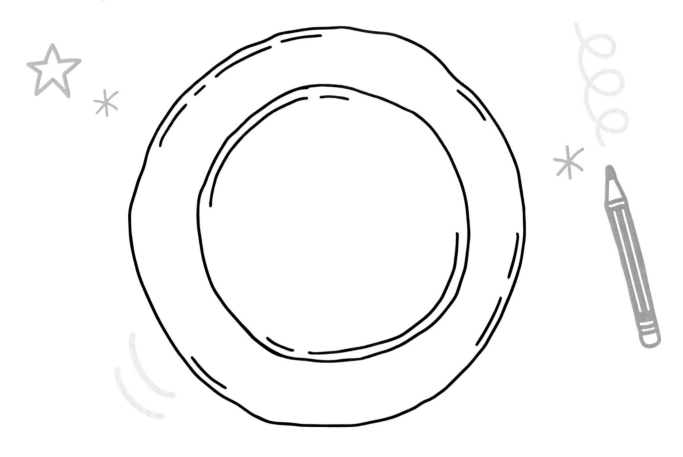

What is your favorite food? _____

Is this an everyday food or a sometimes food? Why? _____

_____

_____

_____

Raising Young

Parents raise their young by protecting them, feeding them, and teaching them. Circle which action the parent is taking in each image!

protecting

feeding

teaching

protecting

feeding

teaching

protecting

feeding

teaching

protecting

feeding

teaching

protecting

feeding

teaching

protecting

feeding

teaching

Answers on p. 127.

Growing Bigger

Write numbers next to the pictures below to show how a strawberry grows. Number 1 should show what comes first. Number 4 should show what comes last.

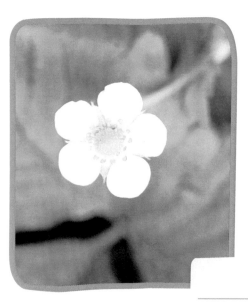

Answers on p. 127.

How do you grow? Draw pictures of yourself as you grow from a baby to an adult.

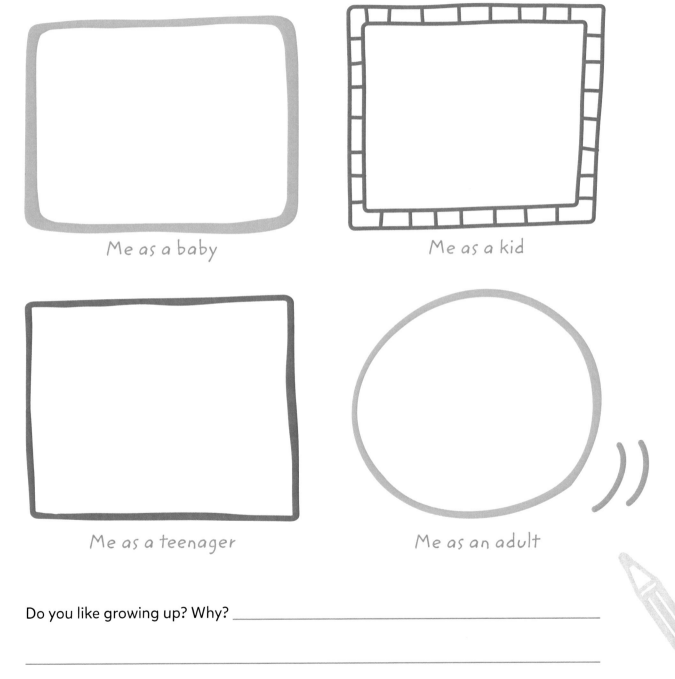

Me as a baby

Me as a kid

Me as a teenager

Me as an adult

Do you like growing up? Why? _____

_____

_____

Pine Cone Protection

Pine cones close their scales when it is wet outside. This protects the seeds inside. Pine cones open their scales when it is dry outside. This way, the seeds can be carried by the wind and travel far.

Label the images below using words from the word bank.

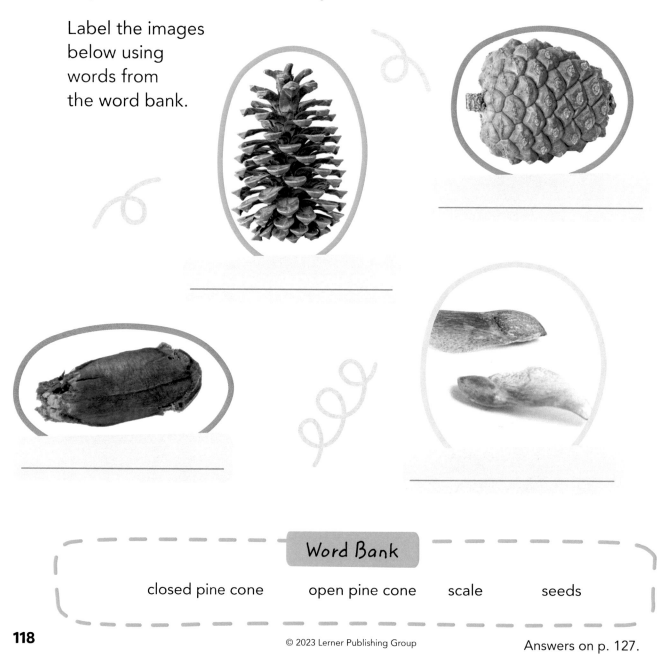

Word Bank

closed pine cone   open pine cone   scale   seeds

Answers on p. 127.

What is something you would like to protect? Draw a case or other object that could protect your item. Think about how pine cones work as you come up with your idea.

This protects my _____.

Wildlife Search

Go for a walk around your community. Look for plants and animals. If you see an item listed below, check it off. Try to check off at least five of the items. Then draw the items you saw on the next page.

Items to Look For

- ☐ A leaf with smooth edges
- ☐ A leaf with pointy edges
- ☐ A furry animal
- ☐ A bird
- ☐ A bug with six legs

- ☐ A pine cone
- ☐ An animal in a tree
- ☐ An animal in a bush
- ☐ A flower
- ☐ A weed

120

Draw what you saw below!

Plants We Eat

Humans eat all kinds of plants. We grow these plants on farms and in gardens. Match the picture of the plant with the picture of the food we eat.

© 2023 Lerner Publishing Group

Answers on p. 127.

Talking Drums

The sound of drums can be heard miles away! In Ghana and other West African countries, people use drums to send messages.

Talking drums are a special type of drum. This drum's features allow it to sound like a human talking when it is played.

Draw a picture of one way you talk to faraway friends and family.

CASEL Domain	Activity Title	Page
Responsible Decision-Making	From Here to There	104
	Animal Inspiration	108
Self-Management	Healthy Food Shapes	22
	My Meal	25
	Tangram Creations	40
	Josie's Juneteenth	48
	Time to Celebrate!	49
	Length & Weight	50
	Tracking Tortillas	64
	Diwali Sweets	70
	Winter & Summer	88
	My Moon Journal	92
	What a Bean Needs	107
	Food for My Body	113
Social Awareness	Color a Kinara	6
	Counting through the Seasons	8
	Community Counting	14
	Totem Poles by Tens	16
	How Many?	18
	No Shape Like Home	26
	Draw the Shape	30
	Sign Shapes	32
	Country Flags	33
	Spot the Differences	38
	Comparing Creatures	44
	How We Go to School	56
	Happy Harvest Place Value	60
	Visit a Coral Reef!	74
	Pueblo Homes	79
	Constellation Exploration	86
	Moon Phases	90
	Animal Engineers	100
	Wildlife Search	120

Answers

p. 6

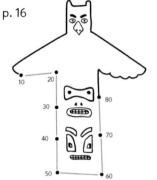

7 candles

p. 7

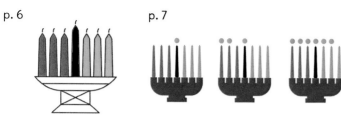

pp. 8–11

3 cherry blossoms

4 colored powders

3½ apples

9 sugar skulls

5 diyas

8 pumpkins

10 yams

pp. 12–13

Amaya; 5 letters

Dolores; 7 letters

Mohammed; 8 letters

pp. 14–15

17 letters

11 helmets

18 stops

12 bandages

p. 16

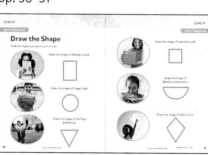

pp. 18–19

9

12

6

6

8

pp. 20–21

the same number of carrots as

more cards than

the same number of flags as

more books than

p. 22

orange

cheese

cereal

egg

p. 26

Apartment Building: rectangles, squares

A-Frame Cabin: triangle, rectangles, squares

Yurt: circle, square

p. 27

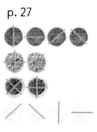

pp. 28–29

above

below

beside

in front of

behind

next to

pp. 30–31

p. 32

Top left: circle

Top right: rectangle

Middle left: triangle

Middle right: square

Bottom left: circle

Bottom right: rectangle

p. 33

Flag of Niger

Flag of Liberia, flag of Chile

Flag of the United Kingdom

Flag of the United Kingdom, flag of Chile, flag of Niger, flag of Liberia

p. 37

1. 4 pieces

2. 2 pieces

3. 2 pieces

4. 8 people

pp. 38–39

pp. 44–47

Giraffe: 20 feet
Elephant: 14 feet
Giraffe

Amazonian Manatee: 9 feet
Orinoco Crocodile: 16 feet
Orinoco Crocodile

Polar Bear: 1,000 pounds
Florida Panther: 150 pounds
Polar bear

Tiger: 400 pounds
Giant Panda: 200 pounds
Giant Panda

Pygmy Possum: 4 inches
Bilby: 20 inches
Pygmy possum

Blue Whale: 80 feet
Fin Whale: 65 feet
Blue whale

p. 48

Parade: 10:00 a.m.

Juneteenth Festival: 12:00 p.m.

Family Barbecue: 5:00 p.m.

Fireworks: 10:00 p.m.

pp. 50–51

Cricket ball

Ping-Pong paddle

Stand-up paddleboard

Basketball

pp. 52–53

bigger, smaller

taller, shorter

lighter, heavier

thinner, thicker

longer, shorter

pp. 54–55

8

6

7

9

10

p. 57

6 students

12 students

8 students

26 students

4 more students

2 fewer students

p. 59

pp. 60–61

1, 5

1, 2

1, 6

1, 9

pp. 62–63

2

4

5

5

1

pp. 64–65

12	7 circles
18	1 line, 5 circles
25	2 lines, 3 circles
31	3 lines, 7 circles
43	4 lines, 4 circles

pp. 66–67

1. 11 tomatoes

2. 7 ears of corn

3. 16 carrot seeds

4. 5 baskets

5. 5 pumpkins

pp. 68–69

$2 + 2 = 4$

$10 - 5 = 5$

$5 + 3 = 8$

$10 - 6 = 4$

$4 + 2 = 6$

pp. 70–71

Sandesh: 5

Pista Kalakand: 2

Peda: 6

Mysore Pak: 4

Rose Ladoo: 8

Gulab Jamun: 3

pp. 72–73

1. 9 dishes

2. 12 shirts

3. 8 signs

4. 18 cans

5. 12 rice cakes

p. 74

p. 76

Left to right: circle (reduce), square (reuse), star (recycle)

p. 80

p. 83

p. 88

June 20

December 21

summer

winter

p. 91

Hilo: E

Kūkahi: G

'Olekūlua: F

Olekūkolu: D

Hoku: C

Lā'aupau: B

'Olekūkahi: A

Kāloapau: H

Muku: I

p. 101

Termite: C

Weaverbird: D

Bee: A

Beaver: B

p. 103

Top left: C

Top right: D

Bottom left: A

Bottom right: B

p. 105

p. 107

p. 110

p. 112

Grass

Hay

Grains

An orange

pp. 114–115

feeding

teaching

protecting

teaching

feeding

protecting

p. 116

1: bottom right

2: top left

3: bottom left

4: top right

p. 118

Top left: open pine cone

Top right: closed pine cone

Bottom left: scale

Bottom right: seeds

p. 122

Acknowledgments

The images in this book are used with the permission of: © Pinky Rabbit/Shutterstock Images, p. 1; © Mighty Media, Inc., pp. 2, 40, 45 (ruler), 46 (ruler), 47 (ruler), 51 (ruler); © SDI Productions/iStockphoto, pp. 3, 15 (bus driver), 30 (middle); © FatCamera/iStockphoto, pp. 5, 29 (bottom); © dbayan/Shutterstock Images, p. 6; © 5 second Studio/Shutterstock Images, p. 8 (powders); © HardtIllustrations/Shutterstock Images, p. 7; © oksana2010/Shutterstock Images, p. 8 (flowers); © Sarycheva Olesia/Shutterstock Images, p. 8 (apples); © Callipso88/Shutterstock Images, p. 9 (horses); © ElenaBaryshnikova/Shutterstock Images, p. 9 (high-heel shoes); © jlbuyz/Shutterstock Images, p. 9 (dragons); © Taras Kvakush/Shutterstock Images, p. 9 (black shoes); © Tartila/Shutterstock Images, p. 9 (rainbows); © Tutamaro/Shutterstock Images, p. 9 (black and tan shoes); © Fer Gregory/Shutterstock Images, p. 10 (sugar skulls); © JIANG HONGYAN/Shutterstock Images, p. 10 (cookies); © New Africa/Shutterstock Images, p. 10 (diyas); © Yellowj/Shutterstock Images, p. 10 (pumpkins); © aquariagirl1970/Shutterstock Images, p. 11 (crowns); © Moran Jacobson/Shutterstock Images, p. 11 (coins); © Noppasin Wongchum/Shutterstock Images, p. 11 (fireworks); © Winai Tepsuttinun/Shutterstock Images, p. 11 (lights); © ESB Professional/Shutterstock Images, pp. 12 (top right), 110 (child); © Rido/Shutterstock Images, p. 12 (bottom left); © Shyamalamuralinath/Shutterstock Images, p. 12 (top left); © wavebreakmedia/Shutterstock Images, p. 12 (bottom right); © mangpor2004/Shutterstock Images, p. 13 (top left); © MIA Studio/Shutterstock Images, p. 13 (top right); © ShineTerra/Shutterstock Images, p. 13 (bottom); © koya979/Shutterstock Images, p. 14 (helmet); © Monkey Business Images/Shutterstock Images, p. 14 (letter carrier); © rzstudio/Shutterstock Images, p. 14 (envelope); © VAKS-Stock Agency/Shutterstock Images, p. 14 (firefighter); © Pixel-Shot/Shutterstock Images, p. 15 (nurse); © New Africa/Shutterstock Images, p. 15 (bus stop); © Walter Cicchetti/Shutterstock Images, p. 15 (bandage); © Alexandra Romanova/Shutterstock Images, pp. 16 (totem pole), 17 (left); © Denis Kuvaev/Shutterstock Images, p. 16 (girl); © Dan Breckwoldt/Shutterstock Images, p. 17; © chameleonseye/iStockphoto, p. 18 (menorah); © phi2/iStockphoto, p. 18 (tomatoes); © Arundhati Sathe/iStockphoto, p. 19 (Diwali); © kate_sept2004/iStockphoto, p. 19 (cookies); © Marco Vasquez/iStockphoto, p. 19 (tortillas); © GlobalStock/iStockphoto, p. 20 (cards); © Peakstock/Shutterstock Images, p. 20 (vegetables); © goc/iStockphoto, p. 21 (flags); © Weekend Images Inc./iStockphoto, p. 21 (books); © azure1/Shutterstock Images, pp. 22 (fish), 54 (fork); © Gavran333/Shutterstock Images, p. 22 (lettuce); © Jiri Miklo/Shutterstock Images, p. 22 (pineapple); © Maks Narodenko/Shutterstock Images, pp. 22 (strawberry, orange), 61 (mangoes); © Pineapple studio/Shutterstock Images, p. 22 (egg); © Ratikova/Shutterstock Images, p. 22 (bread); © SAKORNJ/Shutterstock Images, p. 22 (beans); © SizeSquares/Shutterstock Images, p. 22 (almond); © Tim UR/Shutterstock Images, p. 22 (cheese); © Valentina Razumova/Shutterstock Images, p. 22 (carrot); © Visual Generation/Shutterstock Images, p. 25; © Anastasios71/Shutterstock Images, p. 26 (apartment); © oc_eye_in_the_sky/Shutterstock Images, p. 26 (yurt); © Sean Jorg/Shutterstock Images, p. 26 (cabin); © Glenn Price/Shutterstock Images, p. 27 (pie); © Moving Moment/Shutterstock Images, p. 27 (tortilla); © Nail Bikbaev/Shutterstock Images, p. 27 (pizza); © pr2is/Shutterstock Images, p. 27 (injera); © aldomurillo/iStockphoto, p. 28 (middle); © Kong Ding Chek/iStockphoto, p. 28 (top); © Ridofranz/iStockphoto, p. 28 (bottom); © DragonImages/iStockphoto, p. 29 (top); © Drazen Zigic/iStockphoto, p. 29 (middle); © FluxFactory/iStockphoto, p. 30 (bottom); © Prostock-Studio/iStockphoto, p. 30 (top); © AaronAmat/iStockphoto, pp. 31 (top), 69 (top right); © kali9/iStockphoto, pp. 31 (bottom), 53 (middle), 122 (eating corn); © Wavebreakmedia/iStockphoto, p. 31 (middle); © georgeclerk/iStockphoto, p. 32 (bottom left); © gionnixxx/iStockphoto, p. 32 (top right); © guenterguni/iStockphoto, p. 32 (bottom right); © Harry Wedzinga/iStockphoto, p. 32 (middle right); © istanbulimage/iStockphoto, p. 32 (bottom left); © Stephan Zabel/iStockphoto, p. 32 (top left); © Gil C/Shutterstock Images, pp. 33 (Chile flag, Liberia flag); © Julinzy/Shutterstock Images, p. 33 (Niger flag); © MATULEE/Shutterstock Images, p. 33 (UK flag); © N.Vector Design/Shutterstock Images, p. 34; © BigNazik/iStockphoto, p. 35 (green pepper); © hongquang09/iStockphoto, p. 35 (mushrooms); © mphillips007/iStockphoto, p. 35 (pepperoni); © Veronika Ryabova/iStockphoto, p. 35 (onion); © Mim_illustrations/Shutterstock Images, p. 38; © Nadzeya_Dzivakova/iStockphoto, p. 39; © Mironov Konstantin/Shutterstock Images, p. 41; © jaroslava V/Shutterstock Images, p. 44 (giraffe); © Patryk Kosmider/Shutterstock Images, p. 44 (elephant); © BearFotos/Shutterstock Images, p. 45 (polar bear); © Kolonko/Shutterstock Images, pp. 45 (scale), 46 (scale), 50 (scale); © Pixabay/Stockvault, p. 45 (crocodile); © Svetlana Foote/Shutterstock Images, p. 45 (panther); © tristan tan/Shutterstock Images, p. 45 (manatee); © Eric Isselee/Shutterstock Images, pp. 46 (tiger, possum, panda); © Susan Flashman/Shutterstock Images, p. 46 (bilby); © Maria Spb/Shutterstock Images, p. 47 (blue whale); © 3drenderings/Shutterstock Images, p. 47 (fin whale); © Aaron of L.A. Photography/Shutterstock Images, p. 48 (parade); © Dana.S/Shutterstock Images, p. 48 (fireworks); © Demetrio Zimino/Shutterstock Images, pp. 48 (clock), 49; © Juice Dash/Shutterstock Images, p. 48 (barbecue); © Tippman98x/Shutterstock Images, p. 48 (festival); © 3DMI/Shutterstock Images, p. 50 (cricket bat); © Iasha/Shutterstock Images, p. 50 (baseball); © Michael Burrell/iStockphoto, p. 50 (tennis racket); © Mr.Timoty/iStockphoto, p. 50 (ruler); © WesAbrams/iStockphoto, p. 50 (ping-pong paddle); © Cherdchai charasri/Shutterstock Images, p. 51 (basketball); © FocusStocker/Shutterstock Images, p. 51 (soccer ball); © marekuliasz/Shutterstock Images, p. 51 (kayak, paddleboard); © FG Trade/iStockphoto, pp. 52 (bottom), 53 (bottom); © shapecharge/iStockphoto, p. 52; © triloks/iStockphoto, p. 53; © koosen/Shutterstock Images, p. 54; © AlexML2020/Shutterstock Images, p. 55 (molinillo); © Anna Frodesiak/Wikimedia Commons, p. 55 (wok brush); © dearmkummarmeena/Shutterstock Images, p. 55 (belan); © 4 PM production/Shutterstock Images, p. 56; © WESTOCK PRODUCTIONS/Shutterstock Images, p. 58; © Elena Tagiltseva/Shutterstock Images, p. 59; © AN NGUYEN/Shutterstock Images, p. 60 (cassava); © jamakosy/Shutterstock Images, p. 60 (watermelon); © Kovaleva_Ka/Shutterstock Images, p. 61; © Rawpixel.com/Shutterstock Images, pp. 62 (children), 76 (recycling), 84 (girl); © voinSveta/iStockphoto, pp. 62 (boxes), 63; © Anconer Design/Shutterstock Images, p. 66 (tomato); © Tribalium/Shutterstock Images, p. 66 (corn); © Everilda/Shutterstock Images, p. 67 (carrot seeds); © Lana Nikova/Shutterstock Images, p. 67 (pumpkin); © Oqvector/Shutterstock Images, p. 67 (baskets); © ChristinaKurtz/iStockphoto, p. 68 (bottom right); © Riska/Shutterstock Images, p. 68 (top right); © Sasiistock/iStockphoto, p. 68 (bottom left); © Wacharaphong/iStockphoto, p. 68 (top left); © blessings/Shutterstock Images, p. 69 (middle right); © kool99/iStockphoto, p. 69 (top left, bottom right); © nicolesy/iStockphoto, p. 69 (middle left); © YuliaDerid/Shutterstock Images, p. 69 (bottom left); © yelet/iStockphoto, pp. 70, 71; © agus khamami/Shutterstock Images, p. 72 (T-shirt); © olly2polly/Shutterstock Images, p. 72 (dish); © ASAG Studio/Shutterstock Images, p. 73 (cans); © NotionPic/Shutterstock Images, p. 73 (signs); © Sudowoodo/iStockphoto, p. 73 (rice cakes); © bearacreative/Shutterstock Images, p. 74 (lionfish); © Francisco J Ramos Gallego/Shutterstock Images, p. 74 (brain coral); © FromMyEyes/Shutterstock Images, p. 74 (parrotfish); © Lotus_studio/Shutterstock Images, p. 74 (reef); © maya_parf/Shutterstock Images, p. 74 (angelfish); © orlandin/Shutterstock Images, p. 74 (butterflyfish); © Creative Cat Studio/Shutterstock Images, p. 76 (bag); © Zoriana Zaitseva/Shutterstock Images, p. 76 (shopping); © Vineyard Perspective/Shutterstock Images, p. 79; © hadynyah/iStockphoto, p. 80 (top left); © THEPALMER/iStockphoto, p. 80 (bottom left); © Viktorcvetkovic/iStockphoto, p. 80 (top right); © xijian/iStockphoto, p. 80 (bottom right); © FotoKina/Shutterstock Images, p. 81 (flood); © Justin Hobson/Shutterstock Images, p. 81 (snowstorm); © michelmond/Shutterstock Images, p. 81 (hurricane); © Pau Buera/Shutterstock Images, p. 81 (lightning); © Sambulov Yevgeniy/Shutterstock Images, p. 81 (tornado); © Sawat Banyenngam/Shutterstock Images, p. 81 (drought); © AmitRane1975/iStockphoto, p. 83 (lizard); © Christina Radcliffe/iStockphoto, p. 83 (raccoons); © Fabrique Imagique/iStockphoto, p. 83 (squirrels); © Petroos/iStockphoto, p. 83 (storks); © pixelliebe/Shutterstock Images, p. 84; © Pike-28/Shutterstock Images, p. 86 (Southern Cross); © Savvapanf Photo/Shutterstock Images, p. 86 (Big Dipper); © dore art/Shutterstock Images, p. 87; © Galyna Andrushko/Shutterstock Images, p. 90; © THANAKRIT SANTIKUNAPORN/Shutterstock Images, p. 91 (all); © TORWAISTUDIO/Shutterstock Images, p. 96; © ajt/Shutterstock Images, p. 97 (umbrella); © ArtShotPhoto/Shutterstock Images, p. 97 (windsock); © exopixel/Shutterstock Images, p. 97 (sunglasses); © justone/Shutterstock Images, p. 97 (temperature); © OlgaGi/Shutterstock Images, p. 97 (jacket); © Tania Zbrodko/Shutterstock Images, p. 97 (mittens); © Yaprativa/Shutterstock Images, p. 97 (weather); © Piotr Gatlik/Shutterstock Images, p. 100 (termite mound); © S Nilofar/Shutterstock Images, p. 100 (nest); © Sgeneralov/Shutterstock Images, p. 100 (beaver dam); © wisawa222/Shutterstock Images, p. 100 (honeycomb); © jeremie thomas/Shutterstock Images, p. 101 (bee); © Richard Seeley/Shutterstock Images, p. 101 (beaver); © Tareq Uddin Ahmed/Shutterstock Images, p. 101 (weaverbird); © Witsawat.S/Shutterstock Images, p. 101 (termite); © Fotokostic/Shutterstock Images, p. 102 (tractor); © Gary Saxe/Shutterstock Images, p. 102 (dam); © Gustavo Pereira Castro/Shutterstock Images, p. 102 (logging); © ventdusud/Shutterstock Images, p. 102 (bridge); © Brocreative/Shutterstock Images, p. 103 (child wakeboarding); © Fomin Serhii/Shutterstock Images, p. 103 (child eating); © S-F/Shutterstock Images, p. 103 (bridge); © sculpies/Shutterstock Images, p. 103 (carpenter); © EM Arts/Shutterstock Images, p. 105 (seed); © Mathia Coco/Shutterstock Images, p. 105 (green beans); © Singkham/Shutterstock Images, p. 105 (sprout); © Volodymyr Nikitenko/Shutterstock Images, p. 105 (flowers); © ARVD73/Shutterstock Images, p. 107 (sun); © encierro/Shutterstock Images, p. 107 (rake); © Irene_A/Shutterstock Images, p. 107 (water); © Jay Ondreicka/Shutterstock Images, p. 107 (turtle); © Laura Rae/Shutterstock Images, p. 107 (gnome); © Piyaset/Shutterstock Images, p. 107 (soil); © SARIN KUNTHONG/Shutterstock Images, p. 107 (stones); © siraphat/Shutterstock Images, p. 107 (wheelbarrow); © Vadym Zaitsev/Shutterstock Images, p. 107 (shovel); © critterbiz/Shutterstock Images, p. 108 (porcupine); © Sacharewicz Patryk/Shutterstock Images, p. 108 (kingfisher); © Sakarin Sawasdinaka/Shutterstock Images, p. 108 (train); © Gchapel/Shutterstock Images, p. 109 (tortoise); © Henner Damke/Shutterstock Images, p. 109 (octopus); © Alena Demidyuk/Shutterstock Images, p. 110 (cow); © Alter-ego/Shutterstock Images, p. 110 (water); © FedBul/Shutterstock Images, p. 110 (fish); © Floridian/Shutterstock Images, p. 110 (grass); © Islandwave/Shutterstock Images, p. 110 (bear); © Nik Merkulov/Shutterstock Images, p. 110 (soil); © Pablesku/Shutterstock Images, p. 110 (sunflower); © Suriyawut Suriya/Shutterstock Images, p. 112; © Jane Semina/Shutterstock Images, p. 113; © beyhanyazar/Shutterstock Images, p. 113 (bottom); © Dantesattic/iStockphoto, p. 114 (top); © Studio CJ/iStockphoto, p. 114 (middle); © dba87/Shutterstock Images, p. 115 (top); © MarieHolding/iStockphoto, p. 115 (bottom); © nortonrsx/iStockphoto, p. 115 (middle); © Tolola/iStockphoto, p. 116 (all); © nulinukas/Shutterstock Images, p. 118 (seed); © Philippe Clement/Shutterstock Images, p. 118 (scale); © Protasov AN/Shutterstock Images, p. 118 (pine cones); © ampueroleonardo/iStockphoto, p. 122 (plantains cooking); © Debbie Ann Powell/iStockphoto, p. 122 (plantains); © hxyume/iStockphoto, p. 122 (eating rice); © jxfzsy/iStockphoto, p. 122 (rice farming); © mtreasure/iStockphoto, p. 122 (squeezing potatoes); © Nednapa/iStockphoto, p. 122 (potatoes); © Robert Winkler/iStockphoto, p. 122 (corn); © Ajibola Fasola/Shutterstock Images, p. 123

Cover Photographs: © FatCamera/iStockphoto (child with blocks); © SDI Productions/iStockphoto (child with plant); © Wavebreakmedia/iStockphoto (child drawing)

Design Elements: © Meowlina Meow/Shutterstock Images (school doodles); © Mighty Media, Inc. (curved lines); © Nazarkru/Shutterstock Images (geometric pattern); © OctoPaper/Shutterstock Images (scissors); © rassco/Shutterstock Images (science doodles); © santima.studio/Shutterstock Images (grid paper)